NEIGHBORHOOD HELPERS

Pilots

BY CECILIA MINDEN AND MARY MINDEN-ZINS

The Child's World

Content Adviser:
Tara Harl, Assistant
Professor of Aviation and
Faculty Adviser to SCSU
Women in Aviation Chapter,
Saint Cloud State University,
Saint Cloud, Minnesota

Published in the United States of America by The Child's World®
PO Box 326
Chanhassen, MN 55317-0326
800-599-READ
www.childsworld.com

Acknowledgements

The Child's World®: Mary Berendes, Publishing Director

Editorial Directions, Inc.: E. Russell Primm, Editorial Director; Katie Marsico, Managing Editor and Line Editor; Judith Shiffer, Assistant Editor; Caroline Wood, Editorial Assistant; Susan Hindman, Copy Editor; Wendy Mead, Proofreader; Mike Helenthal, Rory Mabin, and Caroline Wood, Fact Checkers; Tim Griffin/IndexServ, Indexer; Cian Loughlin O'Day, Photo Researcher; Linda S. Koutris, Photo Selector

The Design Lab: Kathleen Petelinsek, Design and Art Production

Photographs ©: Cover: left—RubberBall Productions, right/frontispiece—Stockbyte/Punchstock. Interior: 4—Photodisc/Getty Images; 5—RubberBall Productions; 6—Stockdisc/Getty Images; 7—Peter Hince/The Image Bank/Getty Images; 8-9, 23—Mark Peterson/Corbis; 11—Matthais Clamer/Stone+/Getty Images; 13—Arnold Tolbert; 14—Firefly Productions/Corbis; 17—Frank Chmura/Alamy Images; 18-19—Siri Stafford/Stone/Getty Images; 20—David R. Frazier Photolibrary, Inc./Alamy Images; 24-25—George Hall/Corbis; 26-27—Ken Reid/Taxi/Getty Images; 28-29—Mika/zefa/Corbis.

Library of Congress Cataloging-in-Publication Data

Minden, Cecilia.
  Pilots / by Cecilia Minden and Mary Minden-Zins.
    p. cm. — (Neighborhood helpers)
  Includes bibliographical references.
  ISBN 1-59296-567-9 (library bound : alk. paper)
  1. Airplanes—Piloting—Vocational guidance—Juvenile literature. 2. Air pilots—Job descriptions—Juvenile literature. I. Minden-Zins, Mary. II. Title. III. Series.
  TL561.M56 2006
  629.132'52023—dc22   2005026228

TABLE OF CONTENTS

Michael

Hello. My name is Michael. Many people live and work in my neighborhood. Each of them helps the neighborhood in different ways.

I thought of all the things I like to do. I liked flying to my grandmother's house last summer. I like to look at maps and find new places to visit.

How could I help my neighborhood when I grow up?

Airplane flight began with Orville and Wilbur Wright in 1903. Passenger travel became popular during the 1930s. Today, pilots carry billions of passengers every year!

I COULD BE A PILOT!

Pilots like to fly airplanes. They're good at reading maps, and they always get to visit new places.

Best of all, pilots go to work up in the sky!

Are you interested in planes? Do you like flying? Perhaps you'd make a good pilot!

LEARN ABOUT THIS NEIGHBORHOOD HELPER!

The best way to learn is to ask questions. Words such as *who, what, where, when,* and *why* will help me learn about being a pilot.

Asking a pilot questions will help you learn what he likes best about his job.

Where Can I Learn More?

**Air Line Pilots Association
Communications
Department
535 Herndon Parkway
Herndon, VA 20170**

**Air Transport Association
of America, Inc.
1301 Pennsylvania
Avenue NW
Suite 1100
Washington, DC 20004**

WHO CAN BECOME A PILOT?

Girls and boys who like to fly may want to become pilots. **Aviation** is divided into three groups. Pilots can work with the military, an airline, or in general aviation. General aviation includes private planes and company planes.

Some pilots help the neighborhood by bringing friends and family safely together. Others help by bringing goods and services to the people and places that need them.

Some pilots are responsible for flying helicopters.

How Can I Explore This Job?

Have you ever traveled on an airplane? Try talking to the pilot the next time you fly. He might be able to answer your questions after the plane has landed and all the passengers have left. Ask the pilot how he started flying planes. How long has he been flying? What does he like best about his job?

aviation (ay-vee-AY-shuhn) the operation of aircraft

MEET A PILOT!

This is Captain Arnold Tolbert. He knew he wanted to fly planes from the time he was a little boy. His favorite TV show was *Sky King*. This program was about a pilot. Flying looked like so much fun that Captain Tolbert decided to be an airline pilot when he grew up. He lives in Miami, Florida, but he flies all over the world.

Captain Tolbert always knew he wanted to be a pilot.

How Many Pilots Are There?

About 79,000 people work as pilots.

WHERE CAN I LEARN TO BE A PILOT?

Captain Tolbert learned to be a pilot at a flight school. Students study and fly with a flight instructor. The instructor decides when students are ready to take their first solo flight. A student must be seventeen years old and pass a written test to get a pilot's license. A person may need to be even older, depending on what type of plane she wants to fly.

Student pilots use equipment called a flight simulator (SIM-yuh-lay-tuhr) to practice how they will one day fly a real plane.

How Much School Will I Need?

Professional pilots usually need to have a high school diploma. Many have two to four years of college, too.

Pilots need to learn flying skills. They can attend a flight school or take private lessons. Some receive training in the military. Pilots must pass tests given by the Federal Aviation Administration (FAA) before they can begin work.

What Are Some Tools I Will Use?

Airplane

Computer flight plan

Two-way radio

performance indicators (pur-FOR-muhnss IN-duh-kate-uhrz) tools used to determine how fast and high a plane is flying, as well as what direction it's traveling in

WHAT DOES A PILOT NEED TO DO HIS JOB?

An airplane has many different parts. Captain Tolbert needs to know how all the parts work together. The engine instruments tell a pilot how the engine is running. The rudder controls the side-to-side movements of the plane. The elevator controls the up-and-down movements.

Captain Tolbert uses the **performance indicators** to learn the airspeed,

Pilots must know how to read a plane's performance indicators.

altitude, and attitude. Airspeed is how fast the plane is traveling. Altitude is how high up in the air the plane is flying. Attitude is whether the plane is flying straight and level or turning.

What Clothes Will I Wear?

Hat
Uniform

17

WHERE DOES A PILOT WORK?

Captain Tolbert gets to the airport two hours before his plane is supposed to take off. He uses a special computer to learn all the information he needs for his trip. Captain Tolbert reviews the information and then meets with his flight crew. Next, the crew checks the plane to make sure it is ready for flight.

Captain Tolbert is then ready to load all of the flight information into the aircraft computer.

There is much preparation before a plane takes off. Passengers' baggage must be loaded onto the plane, and the plane must be checked for any problems.

What's It Like Where I'll Work?

Pilots spend some of their time in airports. But they spend most of their time in flight decks on airplanes. They may work nights, holidays, and weekends. Pilots are often away from home. Their job isn't always easy. A pilot and his crew are responsible for the safety of many people!

This tells the computer exactly where Captain Tolbert plans to go. The entire flight crew must plan their work so they are able to take off at exactly the time they are scheduled to leave.

Captain Tolbert stays in constant contact with the air traffic controller. The air traffic controller sits in a tower and acts like a crossing guard. She guides huge planes on and off the airfields. Captain Tolbert takes off once the air traffic controller gives the signal.

The pilot and air traffic controller work together shortly before a plane takes off.

How Much Money Will I Make?

Most pilots make between $34,000 and $70,000 a year.

WHO WORKS WITH PILOTS?

Captain Tolbert and his crew work together. The first officer helps him prepare and fly the aircraft. The flight attendants greet the passengers and serve drinks and snacks. They are also trained to take care of passengers when there is an emergency. Mechanics check out the engine and all the other mechanical parts on the plane. These are just a few of the people who help make the aircraft safe.

Flight attendants are on board for the safety and comfort of passengers.

WHEN DOES A PILOT FLY OTHER PLANES?

Not all pilots fly for the airlines. Some pilots fly helicopters for hospitals, the police, or TV stations. Some pilots fly **crop dusters.**

Captain Michael Bordeaux is another airline pilot. He learned how to fly planes off a **military carrier.** Can you imagine landing a plane on a ship in the middle of the ocean?

Some pilots work off of military carriers.

How Might My Job Change?

Pilots usually begin work as flight engineers. They may become a first officer after one to five years. They may become a captain after five to ten years.

crop dusters (KROP DUHST-uhrz) planes used to spread chemicals that keep harmful bugs away from crops

military carrier (MIL-uh-tayr-ee KAYR-ee-uhr) a ship long enough to act as a runway for planes

I WANT TO BE A PILOT!

I think being a pilot would be a great way to be a neighborhood helper. Someday I may be the person flying your plane!

Prepare for takeoff! One day you may be flying people around the world!

Is This Job Growing?

The need for pilots will grow as fast as other jobs.

WHY DON'T YOU TRY BEING A PILOT?

Do you think you would like to be a pilot? Pilots usually use computers to figure distances between cities, but see if you can do this on your own. Look at a map of the United States. Can you find Saint Louis, Missouri? Can you find Orlando, Florida?

It is 1,000 miles (1,600 kilometers) between Saint Louis and

Orlando. If a plane is flying 500 miles (800 km) per hour, how long will it take to get from Saint Louis to Orlando? (See page 32 for the answer.)

(See page 32 for the answer.)

Pilots need to be good at reading maps. They also need to be able to figure out the distance between cities.

HOW TO LEARN MORE ABOUT PILOTS

BOOKS

Blackstone, Stella. *I Wish I Were a Pilot*. Cambridge, Mass.: Barefoot Books, 2005.

Liebman, Daniel. *I Want to Be a Pilot*. Toronto: Firefly Books, 1999.

Mattern, Joanne. *Pilots*. New York: PowerKids Press, 2002.

Tetrick, Byron. *Choosing a Career as a Pilot*. New York: Rosen Publishing Group, 2000.

WEB SITES

Visit our home page for lots of links about pilots:
http://www.childsworld.com/links

Note to Parents, Teachers, and Librarians:

We routinely check our Web links to make sure they're safe, active sites—so encourage your readers to check them out!

ABOUT THE AUTHORS:

Dr. Cecilia Minden is a university professor and reading specialist with classroom and administrative experience in grades K–12. She is the author of many books for early readers. Cecilia and her husband Dave Cupp live in North Carolina. She earned her PhD in reading education from the University of Virginia.

Mary Minden-Zins is an experienced classroom teacher. She taught first-grade for ten years before taking time out to raise her five children and play with her four grandchildren. Mary now teaches kindergarten and lives in Oklahoma with her dog, Nick; her turtle, Herman; and her grandson's two cats, Mitten and Jessica.

INDEX

Answer to question on page 29: It would take two hours for a plane flying 500 miles (800 km) per hour to travel from Saint Louis to Orlando.